R Gdma

KK

THE LITTLE GUIDE TO

BUGS

THE LITTLE GUIDE TO
BUGS

Illustrations
by Tom Frost

Words by
Alison Davies

quadrille

Introduction

Take a moment to step into the magnificent world of invertebrates; a plane of existence where beauty is in the amazing colour combinations and intricate patterns, even the tilt and weave of a gossamer wing. There's grace of movement, too, whether slow and careful, leaving silvery threads of pattern upon the ground, or quick and darting, in a race for the best food source or mate.

Teamwork is of the essence for many of these fascinating creatures and there are incredible feats of strength that even the strongest human could not attempt. Be prepared for miraculous exploits, both in a bid to survive and thrive in this miniature world – a realm that is astounding and surprising, and never dull.

Imagine, as you explore the pages of this book, that you're on a voyage of discovery, seeing these creatures for the first time. Delight in the bold use of colour as each image leaps from the page; peer beneath the veil and discover more about each animal's lifestyle and behaviour, what makes it magical and why, in some cases, the Ancients revered or feared it. Get up close and personal and let each creature reveal its mystery through powerful artwork and scientific facts. Once enamoured, you'll find a handy spotter's guide at the back, to help you identify each creature in its natural setting.

Whether it's the winged creatures of the air that take your fancy, or earth- and water-dwellers, begin your adventure here. The fascinating domain of creepy-crawlies beckons, so go forth and forage!

If you truly love nature,
you will find beauty everywhere.

VINCENT VAN GOGH

Brazilian Whiteknee Tarantula

Acanthoscurria geniculata

LEGSPAN c.20cm (8in)
HABITAT Rainforests
DISTRIBUTION Northern Brazil
FOOD Crickets, insects, small mammals
MALES AND FEMALES Males are smaller than females

Often referred to as the Giant White Knee, this enormous spider takes around 3 to 4 years to reach maturity. Named after the striking white bands of colour that line its leg joints, this tarantula has a skittish reputation and can be aggressive when confronted. The female of the species tends to live longer than the male, and has been known to survive for 12 years. The Navajo Indian tribe have many legends associated with tarantulas – one being Old Mother Tarantula. A spirit being who takes on spider form, thought to have lived at the top of Spider Rock monolith in Canyon de Chelly National Park, she would climb down and snatch unsuspecting children.

Southern Migrant Hawker

Aeshna affinis

LEGSPAN c.6cm (2in)

HABITAT Damp, reedy ditches, ponds, lakes

DISTRIBUTION Southern and Central Europe, North Africa, Middle East and Asia

FOOD Adults eat small flying insects; nymphs eat almost any creature smaller than they are

MALES AND FEMALES Males have blue eyes and a blue mark on the abdomen

Also known as the Blue-eyed Hawker, this exquisite dragonfly in full maturity is an eye-catching sight. Emerging in May, the adult males prefer to frequent vegetated ponds and streams while searching for the greener-coloured females to mate with. Eggs are deposited on water plants where they hatch into nymphs and live in water for 2 years before crawling out onto leaves for the adult to emerge. In the Far East, dragonflies are seen as symbols of good fortune and prosperity, and considered good-luck charms. Revered by the Japanese, they're thought to represent summer, and Samurai warriors use them as symbols of power and victory.

Western Honeybee

Apis mellifera

LENGTH c.1cm (½in)

HABITAT Hives close to sources of pollen and nectar, natural hives occur in hollow trees

DISTRIBUTION Native to Europe, Africa and the Middle East but found worldwide, except in Antarctica

FOOD Nectar and pollen from a wide range of plants

MALES AND FEMALES Females have hairier legs and shorter antennae; male antennae are long and rounded

A miracle with wings, the honeybee is the magician of the insect world. There are several species throughout the world and many now rely on beekeepers and gardeners for their survival. Teamwork is the secret of this charming creature's success, with each hive containing castes of workers and drones, and one queen. With her slender, lengthier abdomen, she's easy to spot; the bulky drones are males whose sole purpose is to mate with the queen; the smaller female workers gather nectar and pollen, and look after the hive. Honeybees have fascinated humans for millennia; there's evidence of beekeeping dating back 5000 years, and samples of honey were discovered in Egyptian tombs.

Madagascan Moon Moth

Argema mittrei

LEGSPAN c.20cm (8in)

HABITAT Rainforests

DISTRIBUTION Madagascar

FOOD Adult moths don't eat; caterpillars feed on plants such as Eucalyptus and Cunonia

MALES AND FEMALES Males are smaller than females with larger, feathery antennae

Also known as the Comet Moth because of its long tail, the striking Moon Moth leads a short but colourful life, living for up to a week at most. The adult moths' main aim is to mate, a responsibility that falls to the male; females tend to sit and wait to be courted. Males can sense females' pheromones from miles away with their feathery antennae. Using its distinctive red and yellow tails, this moth is able to distract potential predators such as bats. Its enormous eye-spots also act as an attacker deterrent, and are the reason for the name *Argema*, which means 'speckled eye' in Greek.

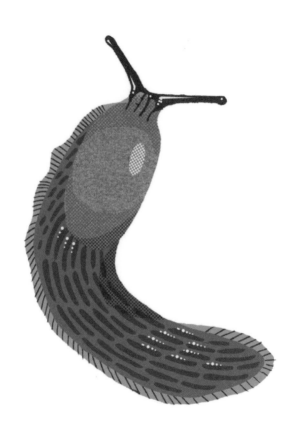

Spanish Slug

Arion vulgaris

LENGTH c.6–15cm (2–6in)

HABITAT Fields, woods and gardens, usually in a damp
environment under rocks and vegetation

DISTRIBUTION UK and mainland Europe

FOOD Leaves, flowers, fungi, roots, lichen, decaying plant
material, small garden pests and even other species of slug

MALES AND FEMALES Similar; hermaphrodites (have both
male and female sexual organs)

A highly invasive land species, the Spanish slug is often considered
a pest. Its colour ranges from brown to orange with dark-brown
tentacles and an orangey-grey sole. The slug is a muscular 'foot'
which can stretch up to 20 times its normal length enabling it deftly
to squeeze into the smallest crevices. Moving in rhythmic waves, slugs
propel themselves forwards while producing a mucus that enables
them to glide over uneven surfaces. Cannibalistic tendencies, 27,000
teeth-like dentricles and their constant damage to arable crops have
earned this particular species the nickname 'killer slug'.

Red-shanked Carder Bee

Bombus ruderarius

LENGTH 1–1.3cm (⅓–½in)

HABITAT Open grassland, gardens, and urban wasteland

DISTRIBUTION Parts of Europe and Asia

FOOD Pollen and nectar from a variety of plants

MALES AND FEMALES Males are smaller, with a faint grey band across the abdomen and a grey or yellow collar

A small species of bumblebee, the Red-shanked Carder is a rare sight and has been seriously affected by habitat loss. It nests in a construction of grass or moss, either on the ground, or just below it, often in abandoned mouse nests. Mostly black, with a red to orange tail, it has orangey-red hairs on its hind legs near the pollen sacks, as its name suggests. Males often have faint yellowish hairs on their faces. This bee has a long tongue to reach nectar from its favourite food plants, including deadnettle, clovers, vetches and legumes.

Buff-tailed Bumblebee

Bombus terrestris

WINGSPAN 2–3.5cm (¾–1½in)

HABITAT Gardens, grasslands, meadows and forest edges

DISTRIBUTION Europe, the Mediterranean, Northern Africa; escaped captivity in Japan, Chile, Argentina and Tasmania

FOOD Nectar and pollen

MALES AND FEMALES Females have pollen baskets on their back legs (i.e. any bumblebee carrying pollen will be female)

There are around 300 species of bumblebee in the world and they all help to pollinate plants; *Bombus terrestris* is especially important to humans because it pollinates so many food crops. All bumblebees nest underground, with the buff-tailed colony favouring abandonded rodent dens. They are believed by ancient Egyptians to have been born from the tears of the Egyptian sun god Ra, and the pharaoh was often called 'He of the Sedge and Bee'. Ancients have always believed in the power of this winged marvel, linking it to love, good fortune and all manner of blessings. Old English folklore suggests that if a bumblebee lands in the palm of your hand, a cash windfall will soon be yours.

Carpenter Ant

Camponotus sayi

LENGTH c.7.5mm–2.5cm (¼–1in)
HABITAT Damp, decaying wood, forest environments
DISTRIBUTION United States and Mexico
FOOD Live and dead insects, honeydew from aphids, nectar from plants
MALES AND FEMALES Physically similar; males die after mating

Clever and supremely efficient, these ants are so-called because they build their nests in moist and rotting wood and colonies can grow very quickly. Those that occasionally nest in buildings are considered pests because their tunnels can seriously damage wooden structures. As a Native American totem, ants are associated with patience and industry and recognised around the world for their ability to work as a team. Even the Christian Bible pays homage in Proverbs 6:6 with the phrase 'Go to the ant, you sluggard; consider her ways, and be wise!'.

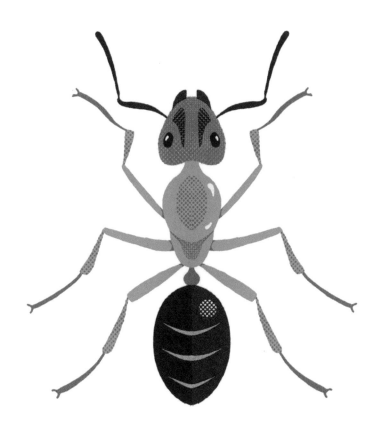

Green Rose Chafer

Cetonia aurata

LENGTH Up to 2cm (¼in)

HABITAT Rose gardens, grasslands and meadows

DISTRIBUTION Southern and central Europe, the UK, South East
Asia and the islands of Hong Kong

FOOD Pollen, nectar and flowers (roses in particular)

MALES AND FEMALES No difference

With around 30,000 different species, scarab beetles
come in a variety of shapes and sizes and inhabit
most parts of the world. While most are either black
or brown, there are those blessed with a metallic
sheen, like the Green Rose Chafer. Oval in shape,
this small beetle uses its fast flight to hop from rose to
rose, feeding on pollen and nectar. Considered sacred
and a symbol of the restoration of life by the ancient
Egyptians, this diverse family of beetles has something
for everyone to admire.

Golden Tortoise Beetle

Charidotella sexpunctata

LENGTH 5–7mm (⅛–¼in)
HABITAT Gardens, grasslands
DISTRIBUTION North America
FOOD Garden vines, including bindweeds, morning glory and sweet potato
MALES AND FEMALES No difference

Like tiny nuggets of pure gold, this incredible beetle (also known as the 'gold bug') is a startling sight. While its natural form is breathtaking, it also has the ability to change colour at will when mating or if disturbed by predators. Some will turn a shimmering rose colour, some turn a brighter gold and some turn red with black spots. This magical transformation is more optical illusion than enchantment, but to witness such a sight proves the power and majesty of nature.

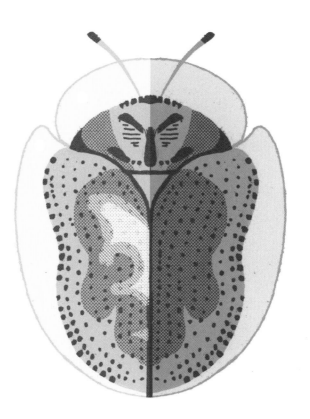

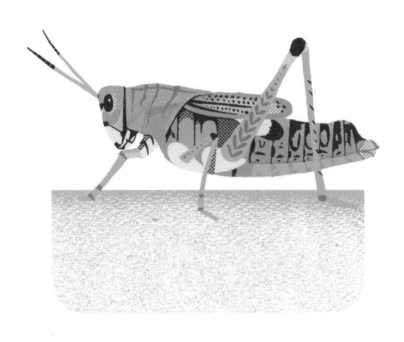

Meadow Grasshopper

Chorthippus parallelus

LENGTH c.1.5–2.5cm (½–1in)
HABITAT Non-arid grasslands
DISTRIBUTION Europe and adjoining areas of Asia
FOOD Grass, leaves, weeds, bark, shrubs and other plants
MALES AND FEMALES Males are smaller than females; females generally have longer, more pointed abdomens; males' abdomens are blunter and more rounded

With super-powerful hind legs, it's no wonder a grasshopper can jump extraordinary lengths. Its two back legs are much longer than the other four to catapult its body up to 20 times as far as it is long. Considered both a good and bad omen in Native American folklore, some tribes believed grasshoppers controlled the weather and could conjure rain, while the Hopi tribe told a deeply malevolent tale of grasshoppers that bit off children's noses. In China, the grasshopper is a symbol of health, wealth and fertility; many families keep them as pets, believing they contain the souls of those dearly departed. In ancient Greece, grasshopper combs and jewellery were worn as a sign of nobility.

Seven-spot Ladybird

Coccinella septempunctata

LENGTH Up to 1cm (⅓in)
HABITAT Hedgerows, gardens, meadows and woodland
DISTRIBUTION Worldwide
FOOD Aphids and other small insects,
some species also eat mildew, fungi and plants
MALES AND FEMALES Males are slightly smaller than females

With their brightly spotted shells (to warn predators that they don't taste good) concealing delicate wings, ladybirds (ladybugs) are easy to spot. They're popular with gardeners and farmers alike because of their penchant for nibbling on garden pests. A popular folk tale from the Middle Ages suggests that ladybirds came to the aid of a group of farmers whose crops were attacked by aphids. In desperation, the farmers prayed to the Virgin Mary, and in response she sent a swarm of ladybirds to save the day. From this moment on, this wondrous bug has been associated with love and protection, and some still believe that simply catching sight of a ladybird in spring means their crops will flourish.

Termite

Coptotermes formosanus

LENGTH 7–15mm (¼–½in)

HABITAT Damp wood and vegetation

DISTRIBUTION Native to China and Japan; distribution worldwide

FOOD Mainly wood (a mature Formosan colony can consume as much as 400g [13oz] wood a day); also dead plants, paper and drywall

MALES AND FEMALES Similar

Although they live in colonies and are ant-like in size, the c.2750 species of termite aren't even closely related to ants. Termite colonies can survive for 100 years; some live in wood, others in the ground, and some in both. Colonies consist of a king and queen (which can lay up to 36,000 eggs per day), workers that build and repair the nest and forage for food, and soldiers that protect the colony from outside attack. Some species of soldier termites have mandibles which they use to decapitate predators, while others secrete a sticky poisonous fluid. Brazilian folk tales often mention 'weeping termites', a reference to the secretions that ground-nesting termites emit when under attack.

Common Garden Snail

Cornu aspersum

SHELL SIZE 2–3cm (¾–1⅓in)

HABITAT Forests, meadows, hedges, farmland, gardens and parks

DISTRIBUTION Native to Europe; distribution worldwide

FOOD Leaves, rotting plant debris, lichens and algae

MALES AND FEMALES Similar; hermaphrodites
(have both male and female sexual organs)

Propelled by a single muscular foot, this mollusc moves slowly and steadily, reaching speeds of 1.3cm (½in) per second. While it may not be a fast mover, it is more active at night and when it rains. The common garden snail will retreat into its shell at the merest hint of a heatwave, when it will seal the entrance with a thick layer of mucus to retain moisture and act as a protective barrier against predators like ants, and will usually hibernate in winter. Widely regarded as an annoying pest by gardeners and farmers because of its love of fresh leaves, it has also traditionally been a symbol of laziness.

Wasp Moth

Euchromia polymena

WINGSPAN c.4cm (2in)
HABITAT Lowlands
DISTRIBUTION India, Southeastern Asia, and Northwest Australia
FOOD Caterpillars feed on Ipomoea plants
MALES AND FEMALES Similar

Flying by day, its bold and devilishly bright display of colour makes this moth stand out from the crowd. Its wings are black with golden-yellow patches and the length of its body is decorated with blue, black and crimson stripes. With a short lifespan, usually between 15 and 17 days, the wasp moth uses the power of mimicry as a form of protection, making the most of its likeness to an angry wasp.

Spiny Orb-Weaver

Gasteracantha cancriformis

LENGTH Females can grow up to 9mm long, 13mm wide (⅓ x ½in)

HABITAT Woodlands, shrubs, gardens and citrus groves

DISTRIBUTION Southern United States, South America, Caribbean, Australia, South Africa and parts of Asia

FOOD Small insects like beetles, moths, mosquitoes and flies

MALES AND FEMALES Females are larger than males; colours are similar but males have a grey abdomen with white spots and no large spines

Often referred to as the crab spider because of its crab-like shape, the orb-weaver has a distinctive appearance – its white abdomen is littered with black spots and protruding red spines. While not the largest spider of its kind, this shape and colour combination make it a head-turner. Most likely to be found spinning webs in trees, shrubs and the corners of windows, this spider adds little tufts of silk to its web that look like tiny flags to prevent birds from flying into it. The spiny orb-weaver has a short lifespan, living only long enough to reproduce; the female dies once she has released her egg mass.

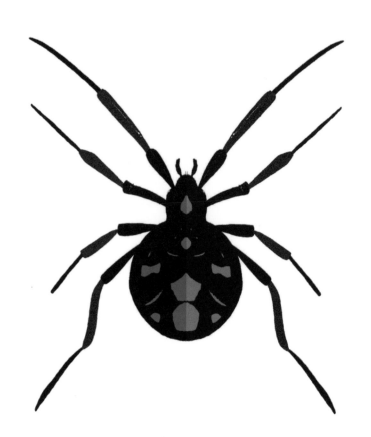

Southern Black Widow

Latrodectus mactans

LEGSPAN Up to c.4cm (1½in)
HABITAT Urban and agricultural habitats
DISTRIBUTION North America, South America
FOOD Flies, mosquitoes, beetles, grasshoppers and other spiders
MALES AND FEMALES Males are half the size of females, have longer legs and a smaller abdomen in relation to their bodies. Females have an hourglass marking on the underside that is missing in males

With its glossy black appearance and neurotoxic venom, which is 15 times more potent than the average rattlesnake, it's easy to see why this spider has such a reputation. This large arachnid gets its name from the fact that the female often devours the male after mating. Deadly yet beautiful, she captivates. Her underside is adorned with a bright-red hourglass pattern and she spins her web in the hope of ensnaring prey. Once caught, she swiftly emerges, wraps her victim in her web, then injects her venom. Folklore has long portrayed the spider with fear and horror but also intelligence and skill.

Leopard Slug

Limus maximus

LENGTH 10–16cm (4–6in)
HABITAT Woodland, parks and gardens
DISTRIBUTION Europe, North America and parts of Asia
FOOD Dead plants and fungi, carrion, other slugs and their eggs
MALES AND FEMALES Similar

Named for the blend of spots and stripes upon its mantle and foot, this slug, like most other slug species, is more active at night. In the day, it can be found hiding beneath rubble, stones and tree stumps, places where it can keep its body damp in order to breathe. It feeds on decomposing plants and other species of slugs, and is seen as less of a pest, and more the gardener's ally. Mating leopard slugs will entwine their bodies and suspend themselves in mid-air attached to a branch by a thick mucus string.

Stone Centipede

Lithobius forficatus

LENGTH 2–3cm (½–1⅓in); 15 pairs of legs
(in other species this number can reach up to 177 pairs)
HABITAT Woodlands, seashores; under logs, in leaf litter and damp soil
DISTRIBUTION The British Isles
FOOD Soil invertebrates, such as earthworms and land insects
MALES AND FEMALES Similar

One of the oldest animals to walk the earth, this feisty predator should not be underestimated. Despite the name, no centipede has exactly 100 legs. With a set of legs for each section of the body and a venomous bite, it kills its prey before eating it. Although a nip may be painful for humans, it is not usually life-threatening but the centipede still courts fear in many cultures. The rapid movement of its many legs is thought to be one of the reasons it conjures such dread. In Japanese folklore, a giant centipede known as Mukade lived on Mount Mikami. Such was its ferocious power, even the Dragon King cowered in its presence. Luckily, the warrior Hidesato saved the day – he killed it with an arrow coated in human saliva, a substance which was poisonous to the mighty beast.

Common Greenbottle Fly

Lucilia sericata

LENGTH 1–1.4cm (c.½in)

HABITAT Farmland, anywhere outdoors near rotten fruit, waste, faeces and dead animals

DISTRIBUTION Common in temperate and tropical regions

FOOD Larvae (maggots) feed on decomposing animal and plant material, faeces and rubbish; adults feed on nectar

MALES AND FEMALES Similar

The greenbottle is aptly named for the stunning hues on its thorax and abdomen. Colours of metallic green, bronze and azure blue meld to make a shining jewel with wings and bulbous red eyes; it's a striking composition for any artist's palette. Integral in helping decomposition, the female fly lays her eggs on rotting waste and faeces, which then provides further sustenance for the larvae. Also known as blowflies, maggots are often used as bait in fishing. Some maggot species, raised in sterile medical conditions, are used to help clean wounds.

Common Earthworm

Lumbricus terrestris

LENGTH Up to 35cm (14in)
HABITAT Gardens, fields, farms (anywhere there's moist soil or dead plant material)
DISTRIBUTION Worldwide
FOOD Soil and dead plants
MALES AND FEMALES Similar (males and females are hermaphrodites)

The soil scientists of the natural world, these annelids consume and excrete their own body weight daily which helps with composting; their movement through the soil helps aerate it and they convert soil into nutrients for plants to use. Almost magical in their undulation, the Ancients recognised the power of these creatures. An Indian tribe, the Santals, mentioned the earthworm in their myth of origin. It was given the important role of placing earth upon the back of the tortoise king to create land for the humans to live on. Until that point the earth was solely made of water. Because of this great contribution, the sun and moon decided that the worm king would be a guest at their daughter's wedding during the rainy season. This was thought to be the reason why so many worms appear when it rains.

Praying Mantis

Mantis religiosa

LENGTH 1–20cm (½–6in)

HABITAT Gardens, forests and vegetated areas

DISTRIBUTION Southern and Central Europe, North America

FOOD Fruit flies, crickets, beetles, moths, bees;
sometimes reptiles, birds and small mammals

MALES AND FEMALES Males have 8 abdominal segments and females have 6

The name 'mantis' comes from the Greek word for 'prophet', and it's clear to see why these intriguing creatures have claimed this mantle – the stance they adopt resembles that of a person in prayer. While this looks sacred, the reality is that with forelegs raised they're in the best position to grab prey, should they happen upon it. With triangular-shaped heads that can turn 180 degrees, and enormous eyes, their appearance is somewhat alien, yet they're considered a symbol of stillness and peace around the world. In some parts of Africa, it was thought to be lucky if one landed on you. In France they believed that a mantis could point a lost child home.

Vietnamese Walking Stick

Medauroidea extradentata

LENGTH 1.5–30cm (½–12in)
HABITAT Tropical forests
DISTRIBUTION Native to Vietnam; in captivity worldwide
FOOD Leaves, berries, fruit
MALES AND FEMALES Males tend to be smaller than females

Masters of camouflage and plant mimicry, stick insects look like sticks (or leaves) which makes it easy for them to meld into their environment. Considering the number of predators they have, this ability to hide is a gift. Some species also use other defensive tricks such as making loud noises and flashing bright colours. After mating, a female stick insect will lay around 1500 eggs, which are cleverly disguised to look like plant seeds. Many species of stick insect are popular as pets.

Water Boatman

Notonecta glauca

LENGTH Up to 13mm (½in)

HABITAT Freshwater ponds, slow-flowing rivers, lakes

DISTRIBUTION Worldwide

FOOD Aquatic plants, algae and plant debris;
some hunt small insects such as mosquitoes

MALES AND FEMALES Females slightly larger than males

With back legs shaped like oars, these aquatic bugs use water tension to lie on their backs just below the surface of the water in ponds and streams. Their eyes, which have been extensively researched, are used for both day and night vision – very useful when searching out prey. Unlike other aquatic creatures, boatmen lack gills; so to breathe under water they instead create a film of air that surrounds their entire body. Although they spend most of their lives in water, when the weather is warmer, usually in late-summer, they will fly between ponds looking for prey.

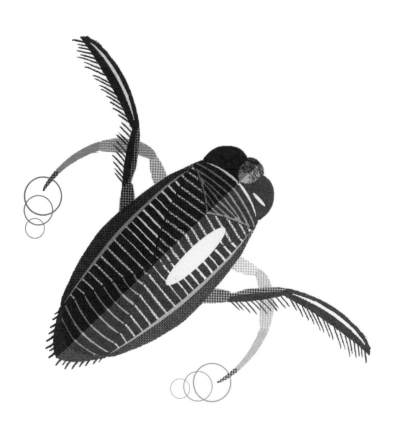

Common Woodlouse

Oniscus asellus

LENGTH 3–30mm (1$\frac{1}{10}$–1in)

HABITAT Forests, woodland, grassland, towns, gardens (most moist environments)

DISTRIBUTION The British Isles, mainland Europe and the Americas

FOOD Decaying leaves, rotting wood and mould

MALES AND FEMALES Similar; females have a brood pouch under the front of the body

Relatives of prawns and crabs, woodlice are actually land-loving crustaceans; they breathe through gills and need damp conditions to survive. Usually found lurking beneath rotten stumps of woods or in compost heaps, these flexible creatures prefer to hide in the day. They have 14 sections to their bodies, which means they can easily curl into a ball should a predator attack. With shiny grey and sometimes brown armour, they do vary in size depending on where they live. Juveniles have a rough shell, which takes on a glossy finish once they mature. They have over 100 nicknames including sow pig, roly-poly and chuggy pig. Once used in home remedies, a bag of live woodlice would be tied around an infant's neck to alleviate teething trouble.

Striped Lady Beetle

Paranaemia vittigera

LENGTH 5–7mm (⅕–¼in)
HABITAT Gardens, fields, meadows and roadsides
DISTRIBUTION Worldwide
FOOD Aphids
MALES AND FEMALES Similar

From the same family as ladybirds (ladybugs), these tiny coccinellids showcase a prominent array of stripes against a dusky-pink background. Like others in their family group, they have a similar oval shaping. Considered the gardener's friend because of their hunger for aphids, the striped lady beetle combines style and efficiency and is a welcome sight in gardens around the world.

Tarantula Hawk Wasp

Pepsis heros

LENGTH Up to 11cm (4½in)

HABITAT Desert habitats, including shrublands and grasslands

DISTRIBUTION The Americas

FOOD Larvae eat tarantulas; adults eat nectar and fruit

MALES AND FEMALES Male antennae are straight, female curved.
Males have 7 segmented sections on their abdomen, females 6

A gorgeous metallic blue-black shade, these eye-catching creatures have a gruesome side. Once a male and female have mated, the egg is deposited on a paralysed tarantula. The female locates the spider through her sense of smell, scampering over ground to the burrow where she plans her attack. The grub will then feed on the spider and once satiated will eventually emerge as an adult. The sting of a tarantula hawk wasp is thought to be one of the most painful stings in the world.

Cockroach

Periplaneta americana

LENGTH c.2–5cm (¾–2in)

HABITAT Commercial and industrial buildings,
anywhere that food is stored or prepared

DISTRIBUTION Worldwide (originally from Africa)

FOOD Anything, although they prefer fermenting organic material,
other cockroaches (dead or alive), their cast-off skins and egg capsules

MALES AND FEMALES Males are longer than females
and have a pair of styli on their abdomen

Fossil evidence shows that cockroaches have existed for over 300 million years; today there are around 4000 species of this seemingly indestructible insect worldwide. Able to hold their breath for at least 40 minutes while submerged in water, the cockroach can also live for a week without its head. It has an open circulatory system, meaning it can breathe through the holes in its body. It is also un-squishable due to its super-flexible exoskeleton. Not surprisingly the cockroach is considered a symbol of survival around the world and synonymous with rebirth and renewal.

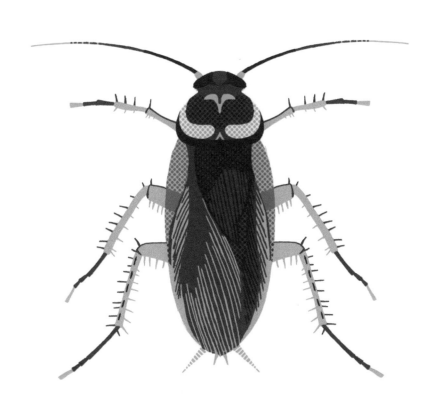

Turbulent Phosphila Caterpillar

Phosphila turbulenta

LENGTH c.2.5cm (1in)
HABITAT Open woodlands
DISTRIBUTION North America
FOOD Greenbriar (Smilax)
MALES AND FEMALES Hard to distinguish between sexes

With its striking monochrome pinstripe pattern, this caterpillar appears to have two spotted heads at either end – a clever ruse born of nature to confuse those predators that would attack its head in the first instance. The true head, which is shiny and black, is hidden beneath a black-and-white prothoracic shield which covers the thorax. This clever subterfuge may put off some creatures, but the caterpillar doesn't stand a chance as hungry birds are likely to smack it against a tree before eating. Turbulent phospila caterpillars gather in large groups to feed on greenbriars; each then forms a chrysalis and emerges as a brown moth.

Eastern Firefly

Photinus pyralis

LENGTH 5–25mm (⅕–1in)

HABITAT Larvae prefer damp spots, often near streams; adults are found in forests, fields and arid areas; they prefer warm environments

DISTRIBUTION North America

FOOD Insects, plants, worms and slugs; some adult species may not eat anything

MALES AND FEMALES The lantern area which lights up is smaller on females

Enchanting and enigmatic, these winged beetles, also called 'lightning bugs', light up as a way of communicating and attracting a mate. Special organs in the abdomen mix oxygen with luciferin to produce light, a technique known as bioluminescence. Incredibly, firefly light flashes on and off in a pattern that is unique to each species. When feeding, they inject a poison which immobilizes and liquefies their prey, allowing them to suck up their meal. The Japanese believe that fireflies are the souls of the dead, usually those who have fallen in battle, while Victorians believed that if one flew into your home, it was an omen of sudden death.

Lily Moth

Polytela gloriosae

WINGSPAN c.3cm (1⅛in)
HABITAT Gardens, woodland, marshland
DISTRIBUTION India and Sri Lanka
FOOD Lilies, amaryllis and crinums
MALES AND FEMALES No difference

With a rich, velvety appearance, this multicoloured beauty boasts shades of pink, white and yellow against a soft, inky backdrop – a true miracle of nature when you consider this moth is born from a black caterpillar with an array of white and orange polka dots. Lily moths tend to lay their eggs on a specific group of host plants. In doing this they've formed a close working relationship, whereby the moths become the plants' sole pollinators.

Large Red Damselfly

Pyrrhosoma nymphula

LENGTH c.3cm (1⅛in)

HABITAT Grassland, woodland, gardens; near the edge
of ponds, lakes and rivers (except fast-flowing)

DISTRIBUTION Europe, with some found in North Africa and Western Asia

FOOD Small insects

MALES AND FEMALES The colour varies on
females from mostly red to mostly black

A sign that spring has sprung, this delicate damselfly
is often the first of its kind to be seen as the seasons
change. Males are brightly hued and can be aggressive,
particularly when other males enter their territory. With
long, thin bodies, these damselflies rest with closed wings
to give them their slender appearance. This also makes
it easy to distinguish them from dragonflies, which rest
open-winged. When mating, the male and female form
a circular shape known as a 'mating wheel'.

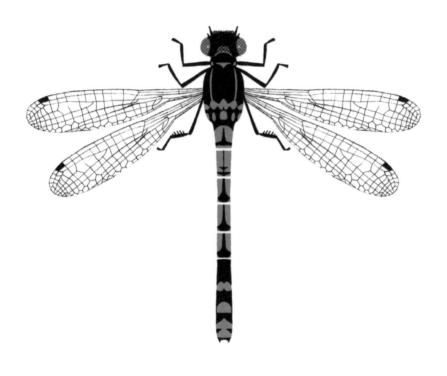

Eastern Lubber Grasshopper

Romalea microptera

LENGTH Up to 7.5cm (3in)
HABITAT Pine woods, weedy fields, roadsides, gardens
DISTRIBUTION Southeastern and south-central United States
FOOD Broadleaf plants and grasses
MALES AND FEMALES Males are usually smaller than the females

Like a burst of summer sunshine, the gorgeous mix of fiery orange, red and yellow that adorns this grasshopper will brighten any day. While it is stunning to behold, this blend of hues is a hint for predators of its toxic nature. The eastern lubber grasshopper may have wings but it cannot fly. Instead it takes to casually lumbering and hopping in a somewhat jerky fashion. The word 'lubber' is derived from the old-English *lobre*, which means lazy or clumsy. Lubber grasshoppers can damage a wide variety of ornamental and food plants, so are often considered pests.

Frog-legged Leaf Beetle

Sagra buqueti

LENGTH Up to 5cm (2in)
HABITAT Forests and jungles
DISTRIBUTION Southeast Asia
FOOD Foliage and leaves
MALES AND FEMALES Males are much larger
than females with longer, sturdier back legs

This iridescent beauty is resplendent in its forest habitat.
Its name comes from the stout hind legs that propel it
forwards on slippery surfaces and help it cling to foliage.
Sticky feet also give it the fearless ability to climb sheer
heights. With large mandibles to munch with, this gem
of a beetle is not just a pretty face – it does its bit for the
environment, depositing dung back into the earth.

Dung Beetle

Scarabaeus sacer

LENGTH Up to c.6cm (2½in)

HABITAT Coastal dunes and marshes

DISTRIBUTION Worldwide, except Antarctica

FOOD Any type of excrement, sometimes mushrooms and rotting fruit

MALES AND FEMALES Males have a stripe of golden-red hair on the inside of their rear legs

Ingeniously clever, there's much to admire about this humble dung beetle, also known as the sacred scarab. Able to source fresh excrement (the fresher the better), they roll it back to their nest to feed on. Some species actually burrow into the dung, others tunnel underneath it and harvest it from below. While rolling a ball of dung that can be 50 times your body weight is an achievement in itself, some types of dung beetle use the Milky Way to help them navigate home. It's no wonder that the ancient Egyptians believed them to be sacred and a symbol of renewal and rebirth. To them, the ball of dung represented the earth and the beetle was the sun, performing a dance in the heavens.

Picasso Bug

Sphaerocoris annulus

LENGTH c.8mm (⅓in)
HABITAT Tropical forests and jungles
DISTRIBUTION Tropical Africa
FOOD Nectar and juice from a wide variety of plants
MALES AND FEMALES No difference

Aptly named, this shield-backed bug is an artistic masterpiece, with an exquisite design comprised of eleven ring-shaped spots. The base colour for this magnificent creature is green, and the intricate pattern is a warning to predators, along with the noxious scent it emits. Small but beautifully formed, these bugs deposit their eggs on the underside of leaves. Once hatched, they moult the exoskeleton as they grow and only have wings when they are adults.

Hoverfly

Syrphus ribesii

LENGTH c.1.25cm (½in)

HABITAT A variety of habitats from gardens and farmlands, woodlands to wetlands

DISTRIBUTION Worldwide, except in deserts and Antarctica

FOOD Nectar and pollen, aphid excrement; some larvae eat aphids

MALES AND FEMALES Female abdomen is more pointed

With such a range of species, the hoverfly family, also known as flowerflies, comes in all shapes and sizes. Most are slender with striking black and yellow markings that resemble wasps, although hoverflies only have one pair of wings (wasps have two). Some are sturdy, with hairy bodies that look more like bumblebees. These eye-catching pollinators are completely harmless and a pleasant addition to any garden. They feed from a variety of flowers and plants, including hogweed, parsnip and fennel. As the name suggests, they hover with grace; males are particularly poised, holding a stationary position while searching for mate.

Giant Mesquite Bug

Thasus neocalifornicus

LENGTH Up to 3.2cm (1¼in)

HABITAT Desert

DISTRIBUTION Southwest United States (where mesquite trees grow)

FOOD New leaves, tree sap, seed pods and stems from the mesquite tree

MALES AND FEMALES Males have large hind legs with bumps and spines; females have thin, smooth hind legs

These enormous leaf-footed bugs often gather in groups, which makes them easy to spot. Youngsters are bright red in hue and patterned with white stripes, whereas the adults are longer and darker, with a triangular patch of yellowish white lines. Both emit a chemical deterrent, effective against a range of predators which is just as well, as being so large, they attract their share of attention from birds and lizards looking for an easy meal.

European Hornet

Vespa crabro

LENGTH Up to 3cm (1¼in)
HABITAT Woodlands, parks and gardens
DISTRIBUTION Europe, parts of North America and Asia
FOOD Tree sap, flies, bees and other insects
MALES AND FEMALES Reproductive females are larger than males and workers

This beautiful wasp, the largest in Europe, is rarely aggressive despite its reputation. Mostly peace-loving creatures, they tend to attack only if their colony is under threat. Their stunning brown and orangey yellow stripes make them easy to identify but generally active at night. Hornets build their nests from papery material made up of chewed fragments of wood and will defend them if disturbed. 'To stir up a hornets' nest' is a common phrase for causing trouble.

Rhinoceros Beetle

Xylotrupes ulysses

LENGTH Up to 6cm (2⅓in)

HABITAT Forest, woodland, gardens, parks,
hedgerows in leaf litter and rotting wood

DISTRIBUTION Worldwide, except Antarctica

FOOD Sap, rotting fruit and ash

MALES AND FEMALES Male's horn looks like a rhino's horn;
female has a bump rather than a full horn

One of the largest beetles in the world, the male rhinoceros beetle is easy to distinguish with its protruding horn, which may look alarming, but is harmless to humans. Some species are also called the Hercules or unicorn beetle. The male beetle uses its horn in a tussle for female attention, often ramming into a rival in a display of prowess. Although they have the ability to fly, their size and horny wings mean they lack grace so instead prefer to hide in deep vegetation and beneath logs, emitting a high-pitched hiss if disturbed. In Japan, these beetles are popular pets and two males are often made to battle for gambling.

Spotter's Guide

This bug checklist will help you identify the 40 critters in this book. Tick off each bug as you find it to keep a record. Bugs are good at hiding so don't be afraid to get your hands dirty during your search. The underside of rocks, leaf litter and earth are some of their favourite homes. Just remember not to scare these little creatures for fear of bites and stings!

☐ **Brazilian Whiteknee Tarantula**

Acanthoscurria geniculata (p8)

☐ **Spanish Slug**

Arion vulgaris (p16)

☐ **Red-shanked Carder Bee**

Bombus ruderairus (p18)

☐ **Buff-tailed Bumblebee**

Bombus terrestris (p20)

☐ **Southern Migrant Hawker**

Aeshna affinis (p10)

☐ **Western Honeybee**

Apis mellifera (p12)

☐ **Madagascan Moon Moth**

Argema mittrei (p14)

☐ **Carpenter Ant**

Camponotus sayi (p22)

☐ **Green Rose Chafer**

Cetonia aurata (p24)

☐ **Golden Tortoise Beetle**

Charidotella sexpunctata (p26)

☐ **Meadow Grasshopper**

Chorthippus parallelus (p28)

☐ **Seven-spot Ladybird**

Coccinella septempunctata (p30)

☐ **Termite**

Coptotermes formosanus (p32)

☐ **Southern Black Widow**

Latrodectus mactans (p40)

☐ **Leopard Slug**

Limus maximus (p42)

☐ **Stone Centipede**

Lithobius forficatus (p44)

☐ **Common Garden Snail**

Cornu aspersum (p34)

☐ **Wasp Moth**

Euchromia polymena (p36)

☐ **Spiny Orb-Weaver**

Gasteracantha cancriformis (p38)

☐ **Common Greenbottle Fly**

Lucilia sericata (p46)

☐ **Common Earthworm**

Lumbricus terrestris (p48)

☐ **Praying Mantis**

Mantis religiosa (p50)

☐ **Vietnamese Walking Stick**

Medauroidea extradentata (p52)

☐ **Water Boatman**

Notonecta glauca (p54)

☐ **Common Woodlouse**

Oniscus asellus (p56)

☐ **Turbulent Phosphila Caterpillar**

Phosphila turbulenta (p64)

☐ **Eastern Firefly**

Photinus pyralis (p66)

☐ **Lily Moth**

Polytela gloriosae (p68)

☐ **Striped Lady Beetle**

Paranaemia vittigera (p58)

☐ **Tarantula Hawk Wasp**

Pepsis heros (p60)

☐ **Cockroach**

Periplaneta americana (p62)

☐ **Large Red Damselfly**

Pyrrhosoma nymphula (p70)

☐ **Eastern Lubber Grasshopper**

Romalea microptera (p72)

☐ **Frog-legged Leaf Beetle**

Sagra buqueti (p74)

☐ **Dung Beetle**

Scarabaeus sacer (p76)

☐ **Picasso Bug**

Sphaerocoris annulus (p78)

☐ **Hoverfly**

Syrphus ribesii (p80)

☐ **Giant Mesquite Bug**

Thasus neocalifornicus (p82)

☐ **European Hornet**

Vespa crabro (p84)

☐ **Rhinoceros Beetle**

Xylotrupes ulysses (p86)

TOM FROST
Print Maker

Print maker and illustrator Tom Frost graduated from Falmouth College of Arts in 2001, returning to his home town of Bristol to work as an illustrator for a number of years. He now divides his time between printmaking, restoring his crumbling Georgian house in rural Wales and raising a young family. In recent years he has worked with clients including the V&A, Perry's Cider, Art Angels, Freight Household Goods, *Selvedge* magazine, Betty & Dupree, The Archivist and Yorkshire Sculpture Park. His work highlights a fascination for old matchboxes, stamps, folk art, tin toys, children's books and the natural world.

PUBLISHING DIRECTOR Sarah Lavelle
EDITOR Harriet Butt
EDITORIAL ASSISTANT Harriet Webster
DESIGNER Emily Lapworth
ILLUSTRATOR Tom Frost
WORDS Alison Davies
PRODUCTION Vincent Smith,
Jessica Otway

Published in 2018 by Quadrille, an imprint
of Hardie Grant

Quadrille
52–54 Southwark Street
London SE1 1UN
quadrille.com

Reprinted in 2018
10 9 8 7 6 5 4 3 2

Cataloguing in Publication Data:
a catalogue record for this book is
available from the British Library.

ISBN 978 1 78713 163 7

Printed in China